CHARITY
WITH A
BOTTOM LINE...

Business With A Heart.

Interweaving the best of business and charity
to help people solve their own poverty.

Dean H Curtis

ISBN: 1475182112
ISBN 13: 9781475182118

Two principles I believe:

1. People in poverty can identify their own problems and help each other find their own solutions.

2. Giving money to the poor rarely solves long-term poverty and can cause harm unless principles of self-reliance are followed.

Poverty is not solved when governments, churches, and/or nonprofit organizations throw money or solutions at a problem. Ultimately, poverty can't be solved from the outside.

This is the story of good people working together in humble streets and neighborhoods all over the world to solve their own problems in their homes, businesses, and communities through self-reliance groups.

It is also the history of how two brothers and a son created the Interweave Self-Reliance Model, a movement that is blending the best of business and charity in neighborhoods of poverty worldwide.

To Julie Curtis

For raising our nine children and caring for my elderly mother while I visit developing countries around the world. You have made this book possible.

Contents

————

www.InterweaveSolutions.org

Introduction: Two Sinks and What to Do about It

———

While I was living in Mexico, Carlos, a friend of mine in Tampico, asked me why North Americans have two sinks in their bathrooms. He had seen a house in the United States once with two sinks, and he couldn't figure out why anyone would have two.

"So we can get ready at the same time," was my first reply. He looked at me blankly with an inquisitive look that shouted, *Are you so busy in North America that you can't wait for each other to get out of the bathroom?*

"Mine and hers," was my next attempt.

"Can't you share?"

Hmmmm. Good question.

After returning from living in Mexico for three years, I remember lying in my bed the first night home after my wife and I had both brushed our teeth in our own sinks. Memories of wonderful people living in black plastic houses with rusting tin roofs asking probing questions came flooding back. I had great memories of loving children and talented parents, of tasty meals and spiritual moments. Better people than I, and yet I have two sinks, and they have none.

Economic disparity exists.

The question for some is, "So what?" as if to say, "it's not my problem."

To those of you who may ask this question, you probably have two sinks and life is good.

The majority of us, however, care a lot when another person lacks what they need when we comparatively have so much. So the question for most of us is a frustrated, "So what *can I do?*"

"So what *can I do* if I have all the food I want and others struggle to scrape together a meal a day."

"So what *can I do* if I have opportunity for an education and there are people who don't have schools or roads or neighborhoods free from crime?"

"Send them a sink? Clean my plate? Pay more taxes?"

The people with big charitable hearts often respond to the question "So what can I do?" by gathering and sending food, slightly used clothing, computers and money. They send money to the organizations that show poor children's faces on the TV screen or to groups that go to impoverished areas to build latrines and schools, or bring in excursions of doctors, nurses, and dentists. Unfortunately, the need never ends. The people can become dependent on the organizations, the organizations can become dependent on their donors, and everyone keeps asking for more.

The more pragmatic business types respond to the question of "So what can I do?" by providing micro loans and helping with income-generating social and micro business creation. They believe that poverty can be risen out of, once individuals find their own source of income.

The more charitable chafe over business' lack of mercy. Why should poor members of a village bank have to sacrifice to make the 50% interest payments on a micro loan so that investors can make a profit? Why does anyone believe that business loans will solve problems in crime, sanitation or education?

So are you more of a Charity or a Business thinker?

How long have you been trying to answer the "So what can I do?" question?

I have been trying to answer this question at home and in developing countries around the world since 1970.

This book shares the discoveries my brother Lynn, my nephew David and I have made as we have attempted to answer the question, "So what can I do?" It shares a tested and proven way in which poverty can be addressed at the grass-roots level by using both business and charity principles. It provides several guidelines you can use as you decide how to deal with economic disparity.

No need to rip out your second sink. Enjoy.

However, next time you are choosing which sink to use after a hard day at work, remember there are good people all over the world who can use our help. We can help them successfully interweave the best of business and charity.

History: Two Brothers and One Son

———

Our family's Thanksgiving dinners are often served along with a friendly exchange on how best to eliminate world poverty. I had decided that business development was the only way of reducing poverty in the world. My big brother Lynn had definitely decided that charitable international development is the world's best hope of ending economic disparity and poverty. His son, my nephew, helped us get together.

Me and business

Palos Verdes, California, has great brownies. The one I had on July 15, 2000, at 11:30 a.m. was probably the best I have ever bought. It was the first purchase I made as a millionaire.

Earlier that day, in the plush office surroundings of the Long Beach World Trade Center, I completed a two-year negotiation process by signing the papers giving ownership of my fifteen-year-old company, Curtis and Associates, Inc. to AFSA, a company of Fleet Boston Bank.

Curtis and Associates, Inc., a consulting firm that eventually grew to have over five hundred employees, worked with Departments of Social Services nationwide to find jobs for people receiving welfare.

We created employment resource centers. With a motivating curriculum, we trained welfare recipients to find work and provided computers, phones, fax machines, and a supportive environment to help them succeed. In many of our contracts, we were paid only if the person found a job. During the fifteen years of business, we saw thousands of people solve their poverty problems by finding and keeping a job.

But the time had come to sell the business. After two years of negotiation and work, we completed the complicated sale.

I already had two sinks in the bathroom in our beautiful home in Greendale, Wisconsin, a suburb of Milwaukee. With the stroke of the pen, I suddenly had millions of dollars in cash and over three million in a charity advised fund that I could direct to any cause of my choice.

In two more years, I had completed my employment contract with AFSA, and in January of 2002, I suddenly found myself completely free of work obligations and with access to millions of dollars.

Now, what would you do?

Most would say, "Whatever I want!"

I did. For a few weeks I took long hot baths, read the paper from cover to cover each morning, and tried not to bother my wife. I decompressed.

And I asked myself the question, "What next?"

I dusted off some old dreams. In July of 2002, after moving closer to extended family in Layton, Utah, I took three of my four boys (my youngest was too young) on a month-long bike trip from Canada to Mexico. Camping out, spending time with the boys, and enjoying the beautiful Pacific coastline was a father's dream come true.

Returning with a farmer's tan, stronger leg muscles, and great family memories, I soon asked the question again, "Now what?"

Within a few months, the question was answered when I received an invitation from my church to serve the local church congregations in Tampico, Mexico for three years with my family.

The "now what" question was temporarily answered. For the next three years my wife and I had the sublime experience of dedicating our lives to serving God and our fellow man in Mexico. Living in a developing country provided powerful experiences that helped form a philosophy of what I should and should not do to reduce poverty.

I remember on one occasion a man called me from the United States wanting to give away some hygiene kits that consisted of toothpaste, shampoo, soap, and washcloths. I contacted a leader of a local church in the small town of San Felipe, asking whether any members of his congregation would want some hygiene kits.

I remember him scratching his head and asking why anyone would want to give him and his congregation toothbrushes and soap. He finally agreed to it and decided to distribute the kits when I brought them the next time I was in town.

We unpacked the kits and put them in his office, and then he asked, a little confused, "Why does anyone want to give away some toothpaste and soap? Do they think we don't have soap? Or do they think we don't know how to use a toothbrush?"

I assured him that people were just trying to be friendly, but it did seem to be a solution looking for a problem.

That sort of thing would regularly happen. Well meaning people would bring supplies to areas that didn't need or ask for those supplies. Of course, the people take free "stuff," but they often wondered why others were giving away silly things. Some of these families and small villages even became dependent on the regular supplies that would come from the "helpful" families from the North.

A generous couple sent used computers and supplies to a small village in the mountains of Mexico. They gave the computers to one family in the small church congregation. Other families in the small congregation became jealous, and the arrival of computers and supplies from the North caused major divisions in the small group, and eventually several families quit coming to the church.

In Mexico, I saw poverty for the first time from a new perspective. I was rubbing shoulders and working with people in extreme poverty. Yet they were happy, intelligent, and contributing members of their community. I got to know personally many people I had seen in the past as "poor Mexicans."

Now I knew them by name, as individuals with talents, dreams, and ideas on how to improve their own lives. Many needed help and training, but they didn't need handouts. When they were organized and empowered with ideas and knowledge, they would solve their own local and community challenges.

Knowing people in a developing country changed my perspective on poverty. When I returned home from Mexico I began asking the "So what can I do?" question but now I knew it had to be more than just giving away "stuff." I decided the answer to poverty in developing nations was business.

My Brother and charitable community development

Lynn is three years older than I am and tells exotic stories. He can. He has visited over sixty-five countries in his international development career. Upon graduating from Brigham Young University in 1977, Lynn moved to Syracuse, New York, and began to work for Laubach Literacy. There he began a career that led him to implement reading and functional literacy programs worldwide.

Eight years prior to his move to New York, Lynn had served in Taiwan and Hong Kong for his church. He saw extreme poverty. On one occasion, as he was swept through a crowded sidewalk in a humble area of Hong Kong, he bumped into a large cardboard box next to a building on a busy sidewalk. The press of the crowd made it impossible to avoid, and as he brushed along its side, he was able to glance in. There he saw a young mother, crouched in the cardboard box, holding and trying to comfort a small baby. As the mother looked up, Lynn saw that she had blood matted about her face. Her eyes seemed to implore, *"Please, help. I have nothing and nowhere to go."*

The crowd pushed him forward, but the mental picture had been taken. He stumbled on, the cardboard box disappearing in the bustling crowd. He never was able to help the woman and never saw her again. However, his life had changed, and he consciously decided that he must work in the nonprofit sector, helping to relieve poverty.

Laubach Literacy was a perfect launching pad for his future career. While completing a Ph.D. at Syracuse University in adult learning, Lynn designed a teaching approach to adult literacy that involved people at the local level in developing countries, to help them obtain functional literacy. He refers to this teaching model as FAMA; an acronym that stands for Facts, Association, Meaning and Action. With this learning methodology, he works with groups all over the world to motivate them to develop their own solutions.

He discovered that adults want to solve their own problems, and health, income, and home issues were more important to adults than sitting in a classroom learning to read. If people identified a personal problem and then saw how learning to read could help them resolve the issue, then they were motivated to learn to read. Lynn wasn't as successful when he came in and said, "Here are some literacy classes." Few adults would attend.

Over the years, he experienced many adventures as he honed his FAMA teaching model of self-motivation. Robbery at gunpoint, malaria in Uganda, prison in Panama for organizing people were all part of Lynn's learning process. This led to understanding learner motivation as an integral part of international development.

At many family gatherings, we would discuss poverty and how to overcome it. Lynn was always very community development focused, and I was very keen on business. To me, without a job or a productive form of income, a person could never lift himself out of poverty. The economies of nations and the establishment of business was the way we would reduce poverty in the world.

"No," he would reply. "Business is about profit. A profit motive causes exploitation. If we can't teach them to read and solve their own local problems, then poverty will never be solved."

"They can read all they want," I would respond. "One of the biggest local problems is that there are no jobs. That means that it doesn't matter how well they read—they still have no money for food. They will still live in cardboard boxes if they have no viable means of income. Someone has to create the jobs, or there will still be poverty."

So, Thanksgiving often became a friendly exchange on how to solve world poverty, with business on one end and charity at the other. Both of us were attacking poverty. In the United States, I was creating jobs and helping people on welfare find employment, and internationally, Lynn was helping people learn to read and establish local groups to resolve neighborhood issues.

His son finally brought us together.

His Son

David Curtis, Lynn's son and my nephew, had a hard time choosing a career. He is a brilliant entrepreneur and was selling Christmas cards by the time he was nine years old. However, he had been raised in a home that was focused on international charity work and was fascinated with the work his father was doing.

He finally decided to focus on business, saying that someday he would be able to help lift people out of poverty, when he made his fortune.

He earned a master's degree in business with an emphasis on real estate. Upon graduation, he worked for major retailers in Wal-Mart and Kmart until finally deciding to set up his own real estate and investment business. We became partners, and he was able to find real estate investment opportunities, and I provided investment capital. While I served the three years in Tampico, he developed a thriving real estate business.

However, he was restless. How was he helping to reduce poverty and give back to the world? After returning from Mexico, I was asking the same question.

Since we were business partners, we decided to see if we could be successful in creating jobs in developing countries. We decided to make a nonprofit organization called Enterprise Solutions. Our goal was to create business in developing countries and then reinvest the profits back into the country to create more employment opportunities.

We started in Uganda, and after fumbling with a honey business and a frozen popsicle idea, we developed a water-purification business. We learned a lot, created many jobs, and learned that international business is hard work. We still have Sparkles, a water purification business that employs over fifty people and provides thousands of clean liters of water for the people of Kampala.

Packing Sparkle's water in Kampala, Uganda

Lynn was watching the growth of our international work, and realized that there was more that could be done. He approached us about the possibility of working together. Although David and I were very business focused, we realized that literacy and social issues are a challenge and that business success alone could not solve poverty. Lynn also had concluded that there has to be some source of income, or else charity can become dependency.

We invited Lynn to join our small nonprofit and began seriously to try to find the "sweet spot" where business and charity meet. We found that with the title Enterprise Solutions, we didn't capture our efforts to help others beyond the bottom line. We struggled with how we could interweave the best of business and charity and finally decided to give the nonprofit that name: Interweave Solutions- charity with a bottom line and business with a heart.

As we blended our experiences and ideas together, we arrived at two very important principles.

Principle number one: People in poverty can identify their own problems and help each other find their own solutions.

Frequently we are exposed to pictures of dirty children living in shacks in developing countries from an organization asking for money. We are touched by the photos and are often motivated to give. We write the check and feel good about helping to solve poverty. They need; we give. They are weak; we are strong. They are impoverished; we are enlightened. Whatever we give, they are grateful to receive.

Let me give you another perspective:

My Eagle Scout project when I was seventeen years old was a clothing and toys drive for a poor village in Mexico. I motivated my friends at South Torrance High School in Southern California to bring used clothing and toys to a drop off point. I loaded the donations in the back of a pickup truck, and my buddy and I headed across the border to a small town south of Tijuana.

We didn't really know anyone in the village. We just drove down the old dirt road to the main plaza area and parked the truck. The village really was hot, dirty, and poor compared to my standard of living.

We thought, "How do we give this stuff out? People are obviously poor and could use what we have. What do we do now?"

By this time we were a curiosity in the small village. People began to gather around the truck and wonder why we were there. We finally climbed in the back of the truck, looked at each other and said, "Let's get started!" We started handing out the stuff. Soon other villagers saw that there was free stuff and came running to the truck. We were quickly surrounded by people clamoring for anything that was free.

As the crowd got bigger, we didn't know what to do, so we began to just throw the stuff out of the truck, and the people just grabbed for it. It was a feeding frenzy for a few moments. Everyone took something free, and then it was over. There were a few kids looking at some old baseball gloves with confusion, so we got out of the truck, helped them figure out how to use the gloves, played some baseball for a few hours, and then went home.

On a basic level, we should be congratulated as teenagers who saw poverty and acted. In this case, we had no idea whether there was a used clothing salesman in the village that we may have just driven out of business by flooding the market with used clothes. We didn't know if maybe someone was learning how to be a seamstress, and we ruined her incentive because free clothes just come from the north. Why learn a skill when stuff just shows up?

Our good intentions could have been economically harmful. However, I didn't know about that as a teenager. What I did know is that I had, and they didn't. I gave, and they received. I am better, and they were in some ways worse. I solidified in my mind that "these people are needy, and I am important."

I came home with pictures and stories of the poverty and of my benevolence. I got my Eagle Scout badge. But I didn't learn about people. I just learned that I am important when I give.

After having lived in Mexico for three years, I can imagine what the people in the village must have thought after our frenzied distribution: "*Those crazy gringos. Drive in, dump a bunch of stuff, and leave.*"

"*If they want to give away stuff, I'll take it,*" I imagined others to say. "*But I have no clue why. Do they think that we don't have clothes?*"

I know what I thought. "*Poor Mexicans need the United States to come down and solve their problems.*"

14

Living in Mexico helped me see things from the perspective of the Mexicans.

That is true worldwide. As the Peruvian business magazine *Caretas* writes, "Peru doesn't need help, we need partners."

The lesson to me was simple. Help people identify *and solve* their own problems. When we attempt to solve a problem in our own way, from our North American perspective we often just fuel our own arrogance.

However, we can also do some real damage as well.

Principle number two: Giving money to the poor rarely solves long-term poverty and can cause harm unless principles of self-reliance are followed.

The harm that comes from blind generosity unconnected to business reality ranges from dependency to even destroying jobs and economic infrastructure.

Dependency

What would have happened if in my Eagle Scout project we had promised to come back every six months with another batch of clothes? What if this had not been a one-time visit? If we had been committed to the village? That would have been worse.

I have seen villages become dependent on the donor to provide the teacher for the school, fix the water pump, provide school supplies, and fix their problems.

Almost all of us have seen citizens become dependent on government programs, people dependent on church aid, and villages dependent on nonprofit agencies. Instead of solving their own problems, they wait to see what the government, church, or non-profit agency is going to do.

It is human nature to accept stuff. If that stuff comes without a price or an effort, and it comes regularly, then we can easily become dependent on it. Once dependency occurs, attitudes of entitlement soon follow.

I deserve the help. I really am poor.

If they are really Christians, they would help more. Don't they know that I can't live on what they give me?

How come they don't help us like they help the other village? We have to really show how poor we are if we want to get outside money or support.

Throwing money at poverty can create dependency and encourage resentment and a sense of entitlement.

Generosity without self-reliance principles can cause dependency but it can also destroy opportunity.

Destroy jobs and local economies

Since my Mexico experience, I have worked with hundreds of micro-businesses in developing countries. From used clothing to reading glasses, tortillas to bananas, each business struggles to start up and get customers. I have also seen the destruction of businesses by charity.

I was working with a group of women in Nicaragua who established a small business selling reading glasses. They helped their clients choose the magnification level of the reading glasses and educated their customers about presbyopia, a condition in which the lens of the eye loses its ability to focus, making it difficult to see objects up close. It eventually affects everyone according to the *A.D.A.M. Medical Encyclopedia.* Most people notice it when they start wishing they had longer arms to be able to move the reading material farther away, and it usually happens between forty to fifty years of age. It is a simple problem to solve with an inexpensive pair of reading glasses.

However, if you don't know about presbyopia, you might think that your eyes are uniquely going bad and you need a professional eye exam with expensive prescription glasses. In a developing country, that means many people have to give up reading or using their hands for detail work like sewing or engine repair because they can no longer focus and can't afford expensive exams and pre-scription glasses.

These eyeglass entrepreneurs offered an important service, educa-tion, and an inexpensive source of reading glasses. All was going well with the sales of the glasses until a benevolent donor from the States decided to help the community by giving away three thousand pairs of eyeglasses. On a special give-away day, the village showed up, and thousands left as proud owners of free reading glasses.

The small business owners suddenly had no market. No one wanted to buy what comes free. Needing work and feeling discour-aged, each one left the reading glasses business, and the market shut down. However, months later, with new people having eye problems, broken glasses, and the need for more education, the village has no source for inexpensive eye education and reading glasses. What was an act of extreme kindness and charity months earlier destroyed jobs and cut off a long-term service for the com-munity. The generosity left the village worse off in the long run.

In *The Wall Street Journal,* March 9, 2009, Dambisa Moyo complains about how aid has kept Africa poor and gives a similar example with mosquito nets. When they are given away, the market and the jobs are destroyed. Later, when the people need more nets, they have no source except to beg for more nets from the outside agency. He explains that the same thing happens at the national level. When nations receive mass donations of used clothing, eye glasses, doctor care etc. without proper technical and business training, the foreign aid actually ruins the local markets and creates unemployment because the supplies and services compete against local providers.

David and I, through our business experience, and, Lynn, through years of international service had learned two valuable lessons: That people can and should identify and solve their own problems; and generosity without business principles can be harmful.

The following chapters share the solutions from years of working with thousands of people in poverty throughout the world. Business and charity can work together. In fact, they must be interwoven to really resolve poverty. With the right methodology, we really can get people working together to reduce poverty having charity with a bottom line and business with a heart.

FAMA

———

If we want self-reliant people that solve their own business, home and community problems, they need to teach and help each other and not always look to the outside for experts. Interweave wanted to create a curriculum that could be self-taught so that groups could be self-sustaining after we left, and they could be their own experts. We needed a teaching methodology that could help people teach each other.

However, people are often reluctant to participate in group discussions, especially if they have little formal education and are uncomfortable with institutions or with groups. Therefore, Interweave has a methodology to get lower income adults to participate actively in business, home and community projects. With this technique, we have seen parents and communities often gather together weekly for years to work together and carry out personal and community projects.

Dr. Lynn Curtis, my brother, developed the methodology, originally out of Syracuse University. Dr. Curtis, with a Ph.D. in adult education, wrote the book *Literacy for Social Change*, and has traveled the world for the past thirty-five years helping to organize parent and adult organizations into community action groups that solve local problems.

The technique Dr. Curtis developed is called FAMA. It is designed to get adults to identify challenges in their community and to take positive steps to resolve them. FAMA is an acronym that stands for **F**acts, **A**ssociation, **M**eaning, and **A**ction.

The technique starts by showing the community group a *code.* A code is a picture, video, skit, song, or something that demonstrates a situation in the community.

Working toward Negotiation and Compromise

Working in Councils

Different FAMA codes to teach cooperation

These are some of the codes we use internationally. The participants see the code and are then asked simply, "What do you see? What are the facts found in the code?"

This discussion breaks the ice and allows participants to start getting involved with easy answers. They are simply asked the **F**acts of the code.

Next they are asked to **A**ssociate what they saw in the code to their own lives. They answer questions like these: "How do the people feel in the video or picture? Have you ever felt that way?"

Next, they are asked the **M**eaning of what they felt or experience in their lives: "What does this mean for us as parents or as a community? Do we have similar challenges in our community?"

And finally, what is our **A**ction step? What can the group do to improve the situation?

Facts, Association, Meaning, and Action. FAMA.

This teaching process creates action that will create community solutions. The process invites participation and helps people overcome their hesitancy to communicate. There are no right answers. What do you see? How do they feel in the picture? Have you ever felt that way? All these are questions to involve the participants and get them to contribute.

What do these feelings mean to you? Why is it important to do something about situations like what we see in the picture? And finally, "What can we do about it in our village?" These questions lead to ownership and action.

When FAMA is done correctly the "teacher" only asks questions and clarifies answers. The real teachers are the participants themselves, who know the problems that exist in the community and often know the solutions if they organize to work as a group. The process can be used to discuss problems in business, in the home and in the community.

Community service motivated by this model is happening all over the world. In Ecuador, participants have cleaned schools, painted orphanages, and grown community gardens. In Uganda, parents have organized small business workshops and trade fairs; in El Salvador, they are turning garbage dumps into soccer fields. They have done it because they felt empowered to do so.

Let me give you an example here at home.

I once used a FAMA code in West Virginia with a group of teachers and counselors.

The code was a minute video clip from Interweave Solutions Education: Catch the Dream! Initiative. The video clip shows kids talking about times when counselors, parents or friends have told them that they were stupid or incapable of doing things.

I asked the teachers, "What did you hear? What did you see? What are the facts of what you just saw?" They quickly stated what they had seen.

Then I asked whether any of them had ever experienced a similar situation.

At that point the group erupted into stories of counselors, parents, and friends who had told them they could not succeed. They were told they weren't college material, or that no one in the family had ever gone to college. They began to remember the pain of their experiences of what people had said.

We then asked the participants, "What does that mean for us as educators? What effect does that have?"

"We have power to influence, for good or evil, the motivation of our students," they replied. Another lively discussion began. People were engaged and involved.

"What should be our action steps?" was my follow-up question.

In this conference, where people came from all over the state, they made personal-action steps. Some were to control language, have higher expectations, and listen to students more.

Instead of someone just telling the educators the power they have in communicating expectations and shaping vision for a student's future, they experienced it. They remembered their past, told stories, and felt the power of expectations. At the end of the workshop, the people had much more than just notes on the power of expectations—they had action steps. They were committed to do something different, to act.

If that group meets every week, participants can follow up on the action step. That is when real community problems begin to get addressed.

Several Self-Reliance Groups at an orphanage in Ecuador

At Interweave, every association or group is given a manual called *Neighbors Working Together.* This manual includes codes or pictures that have been used over the world to help groups solve community problems. The codes will elicit conversations on human rights, environment, cleanliness, health, literacy, conflict management, and AIDS, just to name a few.

Face Painting at the Orphanage

The self-reliance groups can use *Neighbors Working Together* to get conversations started about issues in their own areas and then choose the most pressing issues and create an action plan to resolve them.

A group solution to domestic violence

This code is a perfect illustration of how people can work together to solve problems. A women's group in Africa was experiencing domestic violence. This code helped them discuss the problem and get it out into the open. Many of the women spoke up for the first time about the suffering they had experienced or were experiencing. They were engaged and motivated.

When asked what they can do about domestic violence, at first they said that they needed tougher laws. Although that is true, it wasn't going to solve their immediate problem. Then they came up with a solution. They lived in close proximity to one another and could hear when a drunken husband came home and started to be violent. They spoke of the silent pang each of them had as they heard the abuse going on in the hut next door.

Then they decided to act. Anytime someone heard or saw an abusive situation, she found a pot or pan and began to bang on it.

When the other women in the village heard the banging, they would all join in. By making noise in the neighborhood, soon everyone knew that abuse was occurring.

The man was called out and shamed in the community. Some of the men were also committed to help. They would come over and help stop the abuse. Soon the neighborhood had its own monitoring and enforcing of the local mores that they had established. Domestic abuse in that area went down, and it was solved locally instead of waiting for government or an international NGO to solve the problem.

There is power in getting groups to counsel together to solve their own business, home and community problems. FAMA is a methodology that has successfully improved lives for thirty-five years in developing countries. People participating in councils to solve local problems are a powerful component of self-reliance. FAMA helps make that happen when combined with a curriculum to create home, business and community plans.

Three Circles, Creating Self-Reliance

———

The Three Circles of Self-Reliance

Because home, business and community are so interwoven, a plan is needed in all three areas to help a person become truly self-reliant. These three plans can be developed and implemented in local self-reliance groups using FAMA techniques.

Business

Unfortunately, income provided by regular employment is hard to find in developing countries. Unlike the United States, employers in developing countries can discriminate in hiring based on age, race, or other factors. On one trip in Nicaragua, for example, I studied a local list of jobs available in Managua. Almost every job notice said, "Must be under thirty-five years old to apply." Members of the group I was visiting were all adults who were very capable of working, but obviously over the designated age.

I have seen the same concern in the Philippines, Ecuador, Mexico, and throughout Africa.

In developing countries there are few large corporations with formal jobs which provide regular wages and benefits. Nearly half the world, over three billion people, lives on less than $2.50 a day.

When I visited Kinshasa, the capital of the DRC, I saw very little formal employment, especially outside of the city center area. People bought and sold fish, cleaned clothes for money, rented out old video games consoles for pennies a day, and did what they could to survive. Finding a formal job was not an option in the suburbs of Kinshasa.

Often the large businesses that provide employment require long hours at low wages in poor working conditions. Labor surpluses allow companies to pay low wages and not worry about work conditions. In Mozambique, the average life expectancy is forty-nine years, and the gross national income per capita is only $440 a year, compared to seventy-eight years and $47, 240 in the United States.

I worked with one group of unemployed members of a local church congregation in Beira, Mozambique, trying to help them find work. We taught them job seeking techniques and encouraged them to look for work. One of them found a factory that had job openings, and soon almost the entire group had obtained employment.

Unfortunately, the church never saw these members in their congregation again for months. These members now had to work every Sunday. They rarely saw their families during the week. Over time most of these people had to quit because of the poor working conditions and low hourly wages.

For many people, developing their own form of income is the only answer. Many people, however, don't see themselves as small business owners. They are just trying to survive.

> *I don't have my own business. I just sell tortillas.*
> *I need a job. Now I just paint and fix people's houses to survive.*
> *I don't keep records. I just sell bananas.*

A local church leader in Zimbabwe revealed that 95 percent of his congregation was without formal work. "They live on what they can sell in the street, get from the church, or receive by begging. I must have people knocking on my door seeking assistance about every two to three hours every day."

If there is no way to develop a small source of income, the people must rely on government, churches, and other nongovernmental organizations (NGOs) for survival. Resorting to begging and sometimes stealing can be forms of income that some may use if they don't have a valid or dependable income. If one relative is successful in a business, often many other extended family members expect him or her to support them as well.

It is obvious that a family must have a source of income in order to be self-reliant and escape poverty. For many that is self-employment.

However, having an income is not enough.

Home

I was a little intimidated as I came to a straw home looking for Miguel Hernandez (name changed). I had heard that he had been a very successful businessman in his day. He had organized the local indigenous population in that small mountain town in Mexico. He had a large family that had been a major influence in that poor village.

The house compound consisted of three straw rooms, covered with thatched roofs from the local banana plants. Cooking was done on a fire located in the open, in the center of the three straw structures. The wife hovered over the fire making tortillas, placing them on the pan heated by the open fire made from the firewood that she had gathered that day.

She was shy and withdrawn. I asked her if Miguel was home, and with a fearful glance she mumbled, "I hope not."

It was Sunday morning and Saturday night had been rough for everyone. Miguel had been drinking again and apparently had been violent on his return home. The mother was dutifully fixing breakfast for the remaining children at home, but as I looked more closely, I saw that she had bruises and other signs of abuse.

"We are all afraid of him," she whispered. "We can do nothing without fear of his retaliation and anger. If you do find him, he will be at a bar or at another woman's house."

30

Miguel had been a successful businessman. That had all been lost, and now his family lived in fear and poverty, and he was a broken man.

The second circle shown above represents the focus that must be given to the quality of life in the home. If one gets an income and wastes it on alcohol, does not educate his or her children, or abuses his family, then, ultimately, the family will be in poverty and be dependent on the mercy of others.

Poverty reduction and self-reliance come when the person and the family are setting and accomplishing personal and family goals.

Community

Community problems can often get in the way of successful micro-businesses or quality-of-life goals. In Marimba Park, a humble area outside Harare in Zimbabwe, there is a local elementary school that serves the community. There is a lot of land surrounding the school building, making a great place for the kids to play. Therein lies the problem.

The land is covered with tall grass. The school doesn't have lawn mowers or grass cutters to clean out the grass, so it just grows. The tall grass makes a fun place for kids to play, but also a great place for snakes to thrive.

The parents, worried about the snakes and the danger to the kids, were hesitant to send their children to school. This affected their ability to run their small businesses and to achieve the goal of educating their children.

In a self-reliance association meeting, members identified the problem and arranged a solution. One Saturday morning, prior to their local group training on the Six P's of Business, they donned matching T-shirts, walked the mile from where they were meeting to the elementary school, and attacked the tall grass.

Zimbabwe Self Reliance Group Cutting Grass

Each parent had a slasher, a small golf club-like tool with a sickle attached to the end instead of a nine iron. They cut and slashed for an hour until the tall grass was down and then returned to their meeting place and began to train each other on small-business techniques.

El Salvador is plagued with crime. The big cities fight major gang problems, but even the small communities struggle with juvenile crime and vandalism.

Trash collection is another challenging social problem. Garbage is often not collected and controlled, and is often dumped wherever it is convenient.

One El Salvador community was struck with both problems. The kids were vandalizing the small businesses, and the small businesses in at least one area were struggling to keep customers because of the mound of garbage that was beginning to gather in the field nearby.

Some neighborhood parents who participated in a micro-business lending and savings group received some special self-reliance training through Interweave. They were encouraged to identify a community problem and search for a local solution.

The groups met, and in addition to paying back their group loans, they took some time to discuss the juvenile delinquency and the trash problem and came up with an intriguing plan. First they obtained some dirt to bury the garbage and with the help of the local teenagers, built a soccer field on top of the buried trash. The garbage was covered, and the kids were engaged in a project they cared about. Soon they were playing soccer on what was once a dump heap. The delinquency went down, the garbage was buried, and businesses in the local area had more customers and exposure than ever before.

Many times people in developing countries can't depend on local community services. Garbage, streetlights, and police protection are just some of the many problems that can affect the quality of life and the success of the local businesses. When a community is taught to be self-reliant and is given the structure and support to make it happen, the citizens can solve many of their local problems.

The Sweet Spot of Self-Reliance

Success in business, home, and community is interwoven. If business is doing well, but the family is having problems, success is elusive. If the family is working together but there is no income, then dependency and misery occur. If local parents fail to solve local problems in the schools and community, then success in business and at home is unattainable.

For example, Marie attended a self-reliance group in Kinshasa, Congo. She hoped to grow and improve her grain selling business. She became quite successful applying the six P's of business. She even added catering to her efforts. Her income increased substantially. She soon found that just increasing her business profits wasn't enough. She worried about the orphans living on the streets in her community. So taking the meager profits she earned from her business and involving people in her community she created an orphanage and a school for the children she saw living in the streets. Marie now lives in that sweet spot of self-reliance where her businesses flourish, her personal life is happy and orphans in her community enjoy a place to sleep, eat and get an education.

Self-reliance occurs when good people (rich or poor) are doing all they can to solve their own problems. In order to do that, the community must meet and discuss the local issues. Self-reliance groups, sometimes called prosperity groups, facilitate this cooperation by encouraging and teaching people to create and implement plans in their own business, home and community.

Self-reliance is attainable when individuals and their communities unite to teach each other business techniques, help each other set personal short and long-term goals, and work together to solve local community problems.

Interweave has developed a curriculum using FAMA that helps people teach each other the "Six P's of business" and how to develop quality of life and community action plans. By establishing self-reliance groups people can teach each other, set goals and then support one another as they accomplish these goals.

The Six P's of Business

Each self-reliance group needs training and organization on how to create plans for each of the three areas of self-reliance: business, home and community. The challenge of teaching business to people who can barely read and write can be daunting. We learned that quickly in Africa.

Some of our initial business training occurred in Uganda. David and I had been asked to meet with a neighborhood group in the outskirts of Kampala, close to the banks of Lake Victoria. Our task was to teach people small-business techniques.

I had reviewed my notes from my business training and recalled the curriculum I used in the Organizational Behavior classes I taught at the University of Nebraska at Kearney. David reviewed his material from his MBA work at Brigham Young University. We had organized several PowerPoint slides that could be used as visual aids.

Our cultural ignorance could not have been more dramatic. We found ourselves in a thatched-roof structure that had bamboo sides and open-air windows. No electricity. The chickens from the owner providing the space had to be removed from the tables, and the wooden benches were crammed into every conceivable corner available.

The scent of the pigs, and their occasional squeals, came from the back, where they awaited slaughter less than ten yards away.

Then the people came. Dressed for a major event, the ladies were wearing beautiful homemade gowns that were obviously used only on special occasions. The men were scrubbed clean, and all were hungry for any information they could get from the educated trainers from the United States.

Many could not read. Others had only the basics of English, and it was a struggle to understand anything we said, let alone the S.W.A.T. analysis or strategic-planning material we had prepared. We were ready to present a first-world business program in a classroom lecture format to a developing country audience that could barely speak English and had no electricity. It was obvious that we were not going to reach our group, and we didn't.

That experience helped Dave and me decide that the best way to teach business in a developing country was first to do business in a foreign country. The idea would be that we could start our own business, learn the process, and then draw from that knowledge to develop a curriculum that could have meaning for the developing world.

We eventually decided to try water purification.

Our market breakthrough came when we designed for Uganda a water jug that looked like the five-gallon jug used in offices, but is only five liters and can be purchased on a daily basis for a small amount of money. Delivering water to the small businesses eliminates the need for businesses to use charcoal to boil water. The jugs are recycled, reducing the pollution of discarded plastic bottles from companies that often serve this section of the market.

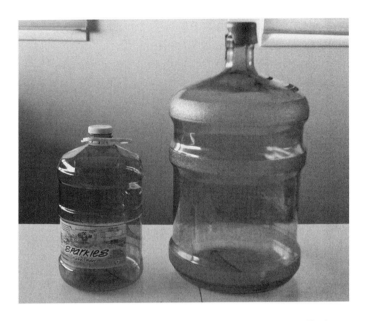

Just like big business only affordable in small shops

We found a niche in the Kampala marketplace. After years of work and investment, we finally received the approval seal from the Uganda National Business Services (UNBS.) Many issues still need to be resolved, and return on investment is elusive. However, we have created jobs for approximately fifty people, while providing thousands of liters of clean water to hundreds of Ugandans in an environmentally safe way.

While developing the Uganda business, we realized that one business, although helpful, was not going to have a major impact on poverty. In order to really change the economic landscape, hundreds of people needed to have or improve their own small businesses. We started working with small-business owners not only in Uganda but in other countries as well. We tested a model of small-business training combined with personal goal setting and community work.

We have since run pilot programs in Uganda, Zimbabwe, Ethiopia, Ghana, Congo, Ecuador, Haiti, Ghana, El Salvador, Costa Rica, and the Philippines, almost every continent in the world. Working with my brother Lynn, we put together a curriculum written specifically for small business owners or potential owners in poverty situations.

It is a unique small-business curriculum that uses case studies from micro-businesses in developing countries and a participatory teaching technique designed to involve people at all literacy levels (FAMA). It is geared toward intelligent people that don't have much of a formal education or any small-business training.

Ecuador group reviewing the six "P"s of business

We have divided all of the essential principles of small business into six areas of focus that we call "The Six P's of Business". They are **p**lan, **p**roduct, **p**rocess, **p**rice, **p**romotion, and **p**aperwork. Underneath each of these P's we have chosen five or six simple principles that can guide the new entrepreneur. A summary of the six "P"s and the principles under each is at the end of this chapter.

"The Six P's of Business" curriculum, as well as instruction on how to make home and community plans, is provided in a kit known as "Success! The Interweave Program of Self-Reliance."

"Success" participant manuals, a facilitator guide, a "Neighbors Working Together" community training guide, a PowerPoint program and flip charts are all included in the kit in English, Spanish and French (www.interweavesolutions.org).

We originally wrote all of the material for PowerPoint, but we quickly discovered that electricity was a major issue in the developing countries we were serving. Many times we were in the middle of a lesson on planning or promotion when the power would just stop and the room would go dark.

In Zimbabwe, we once spent an hour trying to get the backup generator ready before training seventy patient small-business hopefuls because the power had gone off from the city.

In the Congo, we had *every* workshop we held broken up by power outages during the week we were implementing the program.

We also had equipment challenges. Anyone who did the training had to have a computer and projector. It greatly restricted the ability to offer the training to a wider audience by training the trainers.

Costa Rica using "Success" Flip Chart

PowerPoint is a great help and can be useful, but the more economical and convenient innovations that this curriculum brings are the flip charts and training manuals. The flip charts eliminate the need for computers, projectors and electricity, making the self-reliance model scalable. Groups can be held in a home in the neighborhood, at a local church or community center, or even underneath the mango tree. The back of the flip chart is even laminated so that it can be used as a whiteboard.

What Fixed Costs Can do to a Business

The flip chart can be used by almost anyone in the field. It contains pictures of case studies and visual ways to teach business principles. For example, if the boat represents your business, then the fat man in a boat signifies fixed costs such as loan repayments or employees that could sink your business. Any cost needs to be planned for, or it could sink your boat (ruin the business).

"The Six P's of Business" curriculum is a powerful tool to teach small-business principles. It does not depend on technology, and lay trainers can teach it.

The Six P's training allows self-reliance associations to develop the first circle of business by providing field-tested business principles in an easy-to-present format. Step one in developing self-reliance is helping families secure an income by starting or improving their small and micro-businesses, especially in areas where there are very few formal jobs or where it is legal to discriminate against older people.

SUMMARY OF THE PRINCIPLES UNDER EACH OF THE SIX P'S

Plan, Product, Paperwork, Promotion, Price, and Process

Plan Principles — What are the steps you need to make your business successful?

1. **You Are Worthy to Succeed**. If you work hard, you deserve to make money, even if the rest of your family may be poor. Be generous and kind with your own salary, but not with the business's income. Don't be afraid of success.
2. **Eat the Elephant.** Think Big, Start Small, Act Now! Prove you can do business, start small, and grow. The only way to eat an elephant is one bite at a time.
3. **Put Your Skin in the Game.** Be invested in your business. As the owner, you need to invest as much of your own time and money as possible before asking for someone else's cash. Grow your business with profits and savings first, and then turn to loans or investors.
4. **Apply the Six P's to Your Business.** Put your concepts and goals for your prospective business in writing. This plan helps you think through your ideas and helps you look for potential funding. The best funding is your own. If you do not yet have a business, but want to start one, this is the plan you will develop first. Key elements will be the development of your product, process, promotion, price, and paperwork.

5. **Put It in Writing.** Develop an ongoing Business Plan. This is the key plan that guides your business and is constantly evolving and growing with your business. If you have an existing business, this is the plan you will develop and grow through this course. It provides goals and action steps for product development, better processes, successful promotion, competitive pricing, and improved paperwork. Each goal will have a strategy for achieving it. A Business Strategy Plan is a commitment to continually improve.

6. **Make It Legal.** Know the process to have a legal business. Have written agreements with partners and vendors.

Product Principles – What is the item or service you provide?

1. **Know Yourself.** Identify your talents, resources, or desires that you could use to create a business or service.

2. **Know What Sells.** Know whether there is demand for your product or service, and if you can make money selling it.

3. **Know Your Competition.** Determine who your competitors are and why people buy from them. You should know their prices and marketing strategies in order to help you attract customers.

4. **Know and Value Your Customers.** Listen to your customers and know what they need and want. Know your customers' ages, buying patterns, and needs, and work to meet their desires.

Paperwork Principles –Do you keep track of your personal income? How do you track your sales, expenses, inventory, and finances? How do you protect your business as you grow?

1. **Don't Steal From Your Business.** Don't take money or inventory from your business except your salary or commission. Be kind to family and friends with your personal money.

2. **Pay Yourself a Salary or Commission.** Only take money from your business through preplanned salary or commission.

3. **Create and Follow a Personal Budget**. Plan what you are going to spend before you spend it.

4. **Save Regularly**. Get in the habit of controlling your desire to spend all of your money. Save some money or food for emergencies.

5. **Keep Records of Income and Expense**. Write down all of the money that comes in and out of the business and know where it came from and where it goes.

6. **Make a Profit and Loss Statement**. Know how much money you made or lost each month.

7. **Cash is King**. Avoid selling your product on credit. It is like giving your customer a loan. Discount items that aren't selling to use the cash for more productive products.

8. **Make a Cash Flow Statement**. Make a projection of how much you will make and spend in the coming year, organized month by month.

9. **Know How, When (or if) You Should Get a Business Loan**. Learn the four criteria for business loans, motive, terms, timing and affordability.

10. **Build Productive Assets**. Develop product assets such as tools, resources, or equipment that helps you make money.

Promotion Principles – How do you sell your product or service?

1. **State Your Business in Thirty Seconds.** State why your business is better. Identify why people buy from you, and promote that reason. Is it price, cleanliness, friendliness? Know and promote your advantage over your competitors.

2. **Brand Your Business.** A brand is all the customers' interaction with your company. How you present your product or service, your smile, how you treat customers, and the first impressions they receive are all part of your brand. Use T-shirts, colors, labels, words, and presentations to create a brand and image.

3. **Customers First.** Your customers are a priority. Always treat them with respect and courtesy.
4. **Keep it Clean and Fresh.** People will want to do business with you if your business is clean and your product displays are fresh and attractive.
5. **Location, Location, Location.** Locate your business and place your product where your customer can access it easily.
6. **Constantly Improve Sales.** Always be thinking of how to get more sales. Sales are the lifeblood of your business. Remember, you are the salesperson of your business.

Process Principles – How do you create your product or service and get it to your customers?

1. **Know Your Process.** Define the steps you take to get your product or service from your suppliers to your customers. Look for areas where you might cut costs, save time or improve quality.
2. **Constantly Improve and Add Value.** Analyze and question what you are doing, including the value you add to the process. Be faster, friendlier, cleaner, better, or less expensive than your competitor.
3. **Work on Your Business, Not Just in Your Business.** Think about how to grow and improve the business. Don't just make shoes; make a shoe business. Give it your all. Be actively engaged in your business.
4. **Hire Slow. Fire Fast.** Think twice before hiring a family member or friend, and if an employee is not working out, you need to let him or her go sooner rather than later.
5. **Many Suppliers are Better Than One.** With several suppliers, when one charges more or runs out of supply, you can depend on the other and better control your prices.

Price Principles – How much do you charge for your product or service? What practices influence price?

1. **Know the True Price of Your Product or Service.** Knowing your fixed and variable costs makes it possible to determine the true cost of the product.
2. **Base Your Price on What the Market Will Let You Charge.** You can charge much more than what it costs to make your product or service (a profit) if there is high demand and you are better than your competition. Don't always compete on price.

The "Q": Quality Of Life in Home and Community

What seems to be the problem?

What do you see in this picture?
Why is the boy frustrated?
Would you be frustrated in a similar situation?
Have you ever been in a similar situation?
Can you share that with the group?

Just like the boy with the square wheel, we can also become frustrated if our lives are not well rounded.

This FAMA series of questions is the introduction for members of the associations to begin to discuss their own personal quality of life. It is fascinating to listen as people talk of struggling family relationships, not being able to read, or battles with alcohol. Some talk of losing weight or exercising regularly.

The participants identify eight areas of life in which a person can consider improvement. We discuss some of the areas listed below.

1. **Literacy and Education.** Seek functional literacy, life skills, and continuous education for you and your family.
2. **Budget and Save.** Set goals, manage budgets and resources, and save a little each month.
3. **Be Prepared.** Plan for future opportunities and emergencies through food storage, gardening, first aid, and home safety.
4. **Sustain Physical Health.** Eat nutritiously and exercise regularly. Avoid and overcome addictions. Prevent and treat sickness in your home.
5. **Strengthen Your Family.** Spend quality time with your spouse and children. Overcome domestic violence/abuse, and teach your children positive values and practices.
6. **Spiritual/Emotional.** Live with hope and faith. Seek inner strength. Develop reverence and respect for that which is sacred in your life.
7. **Business/Work.** Provide sufficient income for necessities for you and your family.
8. **Social/Friends.** Develop and nurture positive relationships with people who are important in your life.
9. **Community/Church Service.** Be active in your community/church and serve others.
10. **Your Surroundings.** Fix-up, repair, and beautify home surroundings and improve your environment.

The members of the self-reliance group choose one of these areas of focus or others of their liking and write them on the end of each of the eight spokes on a wheel. Each spoke has five dots on it. The association members rate themselves in each area

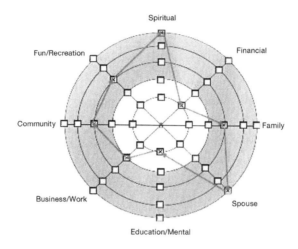

Making a Quality of Life Wheel

As they rate themselves in each theme, they mark the dot in the circle to indicate where they are in their personal lives in that area. A rating close to the center of the circle means there is room for improvement. Marking the box on the outer edge of the circle suggests they are doing better in that area.

We then ask them to connect the dots. The connected dots will usually create a lop-sided circle, as shown in this example. The deformed circle represents the imbalance that the person may have in his or her life. We compare the deformed circle to the boy with the square-wheeled tricycle and invite members to set short-term and long-term goals on how to improve the balance in their lives.

Rodrigo was a member of a self-reliance group in Quito, Ecuador. He had started different business several times in his life. As he was making his quality of life plan he listed health as one of the areas of his life that he wanted to improve. He had a problem with alcohol and he realized that it didn't matter how well he could do business if he wasted all of his money and time drinking. He and his wife were separated and he knew that alcohol had destroyed his marriage. He decided to get help that week on how to stop drinking.

Each week he set another short-term goal to help him conquer the drinking habit. He had a group that would support him and ask him how he was doing each week. Working with the group on his personal goals, Rodrigo was able to take on the real cause of his poverty and saved his marriage in the process.

Gloria can't read or write. She has provided for her family by selling morocho, a homegrown corn drink, out of a corner of the wall in a well-trafficked corner of Quito.

Gloria selling morocho in Quito, Ecuador

She heard about a self-reliance association being set up in the neighborhood nearby and decided to join. She attended regularly and began to improve her business. She worked on better presentation at the shop, and she began to keep very simple records of what she had bought and sold. Her business was improving.

Then the association discussed quality of life. She identified the need to improve her spirituality. She discussed the dream she had of someday preparing herself to go to a special religious temple in Guayaquil. When asked why she hadn't gone before, she said she had never really set that goal before and didn't know how to go.

During the class exercise, she set short-term goals on how to go to Guayaquil. She visited with her local church leader, and, working with him, joined a church bus trip from Quito to Guayaquil and entered that temple for the first time in twenty years.

For her, success in the business was only part of the life she wanted. She had achieved a spiritual goal that had eluded her for twenty years by setting a goal and systematically working toward that goal with the support of other members of the group.

Some members of the groups choose to obtain reading classes; others work on physical areas of their lives. Many set goals to have better communication in the home and to improve their education.

One area we always teach is the importance of home budgeting. We want each association member to know that financial success can come about as much by how we spend, as by how much we earn.

Why should I budget in the home?

This drawing sparks an interesting discussion on family spending.

What do you see in the drawing?
What is she feeling?
Why?

The group will quickly relate to this drawing. Many families in developing countries have a television or other expensive appliances in very poor circumstances.

A lively discussion on wants versus needs will usually occur. It is at the end of this discussion that we ask each person to create his or her own family budget. They need to have their own family discussion of wants versus needs and set personal financial goals for budgeting and savings.

This budgeting discussion can have a powerful impact on self-reliance association members. It gives them a chance to learn from each other the importance of budgeting and savings. It may be one of the first times in their lives when they have discussed how to save and budget.

That is true of the other areas of life as well. As people set personal goals, they begin to focus on a balanced life and not just how to make more money in a business. Self-reliance comes when the association members help each other in all three areas of business, home, and community. Home and life plans are an important part of that process.

Hundreds of Community
Action Projects

———

In the mountains of Ecuador that surround the beautiful capital of Quito, there is a garden. This garden used to be an empty field growing weeds and collecting wind-tossed garbage from the nearby community. Its owner was an overwhelmed lady who didn't have the time, knowledge, or ability to clear and plant the space.

She joined the Inaquito Self-Reliance Group. After a few meetings, members discussed the need for community service. They realized that self-reliance would occur only if they as a community began resolving their own problems. During the group meeting, they listed some of the issues that were challenging the community. They discussed garbage in the streets, hungry children begging at the nearby plaza, reading problems, and poverty.

Finally, the lady spoke up. She owned land. If the association wanted to use it, they could grow some food and share it with the local orphanage. The idea began to take shape, and before the night was over, the members had decided on a community service plan with specific dates and times to gather, to plant and care for the garden.

They were successful, and six months later they had a successful crop that they shared with those who participated in the work, with a significant portion going to the local orphanage.

Many social ills need to be resolved locally. International NGOs can plan from a distance to ship in food, build schools, or solve malaria, but real success comes when the local people decide what is a challenge to them and work together to meet that challenge.

These are the general areas that groups will often focus on to solve their local community issues:

> **Literacy and Education** – We can learn together to gain skills, information, and confidence to improve our homes and communities. Parents can help their children learn and succeed in school.
> **Health** – Families in our community can enjoy health and well-being, and we can join with others to improve physical, emotional, and social health.
> **Physical** – Cleanliness, good nutrition, protection from AIDS/disease, addiction, violence, and abuse.
> **Emotional/Spiritual** – Faith/hope/gratitude, helping others, fulfilling goals/commitments.
> **Social** – Strengthening families, working with others, helping each other.
> **Human Rights** – Every human being is entitled to certain rights regardless of race, gender, age, marital status, or beliefs. We can understand our rights and join with others to protect and respect rights and dignity.
> **Environment** – We can learn and share ideas and simple technologies to solve environmental problems related to water, health, safety, and income.
> **Conflict Resolution/Peace** – We can learn to work together to resolve conflicts with family members and neighbors.

The self-reliance group can use the "Neighbors Working Together" manual, part of the Success Kit that encourages discussions of community problems through a series of pictures that we call codes. Each of these codes helps the group members discuss some of the local problems communities face. As members discuss the pictures, they begin to apply some of the thinking to their local area, and soon start developing a plan they can follow to help resolve the identified social ill.

I have seen many water pumps in Africa that are broken and deserted, with people walking past them to the stream miles away. When I ask why they don't use the well, they simply explain that it doesn't work. Foreigners came, dug and built a well, and left. It worked for a while, and then it broke. "We don't know how to fix it," they say. "We didn't build it," they reason, and "We don't know who is responsible for it."

When water projects are more forward thinking, and arranged with the tribal leaders to manage and maintain the wells, other problems can occur. The leaders decide to "own" the well and soon make a profit on the water. The community becomes divided on how the well is controlled. Conflict can overwhelm the community.

Nearby villages, instead of working on their own water problem, wait with fading hope that an international organization will drop into their village and will also bless them with a well.

How is self-reliance taught when this happens? The attitude of the people of several communities is to appear to foreigners as poor and as helpless as possible, so that the international NGOs will see that they need the well (school, bridge, dental help) more than the community next door.

When help comes from the outside without planning and local initiative, the help often causes dependency. The community is thankful that they received the assistance, but don't know why they were lucky enough to receive it, and the community down the road is wondering why they didn't get a school for their area.

Maybe, they reason, they should appear more needy or poverty stricken the next time the Americans come.

Luck and hope for an international intervention is not the way to create self-reliance. Ideas and plans must come from the community members. When they form groups to discuss local problems, the need for a school or a well, then they can work to achieve it.

If they dig their own well or build their own school, then there is a sense of self-reliance. If they don't have the money or knowledge they need to accomplish their goal, then they learn. They ask questions, they save money, they offer their labor, and they contact resources. They do all they can to help themselves and to resolve their own problems.

If they are fortunate to partner with an international NGO, then they will already have the organization and plan to maintain the well or school when it is built.

Community-based service projects generated by the local neighborhood are powerful ways to increase self-reliance and reduce poverty.

The Need to Be Culturally Minded

My brother was working with a community in Mexico teaching people how to organize themselves to resolve community issues. His international NGO had promised a small grant to help them solve the problems that they had identified, after discussing all of the weighty issues listed above. After a little discussion, they informed Lynn of the area they wanted to resolve:

"We want a Mariachi band."

Lynn, who had been teaching the importance of local control and direction, was taken aback. "A Mariachi band? With all of the important issues we discussed?"

"Sí, that is what we need."

He reluctantly agreed, and his organization funded a fledgling Mariachi band.

A few months later he attended the inauguration of the band and enjoyed the community feast. Much like the boys' band in the musical *The Music Man*, the crowd cheered with delight and pride as the musicians hit one note in three as they played their first rendition.

The director later told Lynn, "We knew what you wanted us to spend the money on. However, in this part of Mexico, any small community that doesn't have a Mariachi band is nothing. Once we have a band, we have a community, and once we have a community, we can solve the other problems that we face. We start with a band."

Lynn later saw the truth of the leader's words. In the following months and years, the community resolved many of its challenging problems. However, for them, it started with a sense of pride in community. It started with a Mariachi band.

Local community groups know the culture and can solve local issues better than people from the outside. If international organizations partner with local self-reliance groups that identify issues, navigate local customs and mores, and are partners in the solution, then the service rendered can have a lasting impact on the community.

Uganda Service Project

We have seen hundreds of service projects around the world. This is a picture of several self-reliance groups in Uganda repairing a road. After the project they shared skits, songs, and samples of their business products.

Self-reliance occurs when we help people resolve their own problems by establishing groups with the purpose of improving their income and business, setting personal goals, and working together as a community.

This formula creates hundreds of community service projects without having to have expeditions from foreign lands come down to dole out resources and culturally blind resolutions to local problems.

Intercultural exchange has a value. It helps the wealthy understand and appreciate their less fortunate neighbors for example. It provides a way to share what we have with those that need what we have to offer. But, unless we train locals how to help themselves, expeditions may not be a valuable tool to eliminate poverty.

Interweaving the Three Circles

––––

We identify areas of extreme poverty around the world and intervene to create, educate, and mentor self-reliance groups. Our intervention provides a participatory curriculum, micro-loan access, and an operating model that empowers self-reliance groups and their members to achieve success in business, home, and community. We partner with local organizations to ensure that each group remains active, self-reliant, and expanding.

Interweave Mission Statement

I just finished reading about one of CNN's top ten heroes. He is an Italian chef in Anaheim, California, who feeds three hundred kids a plate of pasta each day, many of whom are homeless or "motel kids." He said that with part of the prize money from CNN, he wants to inform other restaurants and chefs how they can all work together to one day feed millions of Americans.

I applaud his work. It is necessary. There are hungry kids who need to be fed. But can we feed them for a lifetime? In addition to the food today, we need to help the parents work toward self-reliance tomorrow. We need to create a support system through which the parents can work to help themselves and their kids.

Interweave identifies an area of poverty and connects with a local church, school, or nonprofit organization to establish self-reliance associations. The model is developed in different ways.

Option one: Professional Interweave self-reliance coaches

Interweave hires a local self-reliance coach to work in an identified area of poverty in the United States or a developing country. The area of poverty is chosen by first identifying a local organization, one that has a desire to help their members out of poverty by establishing self-reliance groups. We have worked with micro-finance institutions (MFIs), drug rehabilitation centers, schools, other non-governmental organizations (NGOs) and local churches. If the leaders decide they want the training, they must agree to provide the use of their buildings once a week for the meetings and to announce the association meetings to their congregations or group members.

Once we identify eight to ten congregations or organizations in an area, then we hire and train one or more self-reliance coaches. Each coach will work with five groups, one group each day of the week.

The coaches are equipped with training, a curriculum, and transportation expenses. No office is needed, so no donated money is spent on administrative brick and mortar. The local organizations are already contributing to the effort by providing local facilities and leadership.

The local organization announces the new program. It explains that a group is being formed to help anyone who is interested to set up or improve their business and to work together to become more successful in life.

All the interested members and their friends in that organization meet for an orientation where the Interweave self-reliance model is explained. They are invited to the group meetings to be held one night each week (or day meetings if it is unsafe to be out at night). The coach sets up a different day for each of the five organizations that he or she has to coach.

The coach then works with a different group each day. The coach goes to the poverty area during the day and mentors small business owners or potential start-ups one on one in their homes or places of business. Then they have their self-reliance meeting in the evening.

It is more than just a class. It is a commitment to improve a person's business, home, and community. The goal is to make sure that life changes are made.

After three to five meetings, the group will know which members are attending regularly and are showing leadership potential. In one of the meetings, members have an election and choose a president, vice president, and a council to help plan and organize and eventually teach the material.

The coach begins to mentor the leadership of the groups. The groups decide topics to discuss and organize the community service projects. The coach and leaders begin to identify people who can provide insight and training within the group. The curriculum materials are shared with the group, and the members of the group begin to teach the lessons, lead the discussions, and decide the future efforts of the association.

Within a short period of time, the groups are often functioning on their own. The organization has its own self-reliance group. The coaches' role is to visit monthly and then quarterly to see how the groups are doing. When new members join the congregation or move into the area, they have a support group that can help them become self-reliant. Their neighbors who are not members of the NGO or local church can also be included.

Now the organization is self-reliant in helping its members. It is not waiting for an outside agency or government to solve its problems. The congregation or organization has the structure and capability to help itself.

We followed this model almost two years ago in Ecuador with several local churches. We established a self-reliance group in several of their congregations and invited all of the members to attend.

We established two or three associations in different church buildings throughout Quito. Of the ten associations started, seven are still functioning and are largely self-sustaining. The coaches are now reaching out to more congregations and organizations in other areas of Ecuador.

The associations have provided service projects to orphanages, cleaned up streets, and started businesses. Participants achieved goals such as inspiring neighbors to join the church for additional spiritual guidance, losing weight, and continuing education.

In addition to strengthening existing businesses and starting their own new micro-businesses, over a hundred new jobs have been created, and many of them are shared with other group members. Now the church has several self-reliance groups which new members, friends, and neighbors can attend to help themselves develop their personal plans for self-reliance.

We have established similar groups with schools, micro-finance institutions, a drug rehabilitation center and even businesses that want their employees to be entrepreneurs and sell their products. Self Reliance groups work.

Option two: Train volunteer staff to create self-reliance groups.

Interweave provides self-reliance group training to the leaders of a congregation or organization in a chosen area of poverty. If the leadership of the organization wants to establish a self-reliance group in their area, they ask two people from each congregation or group to provide the leadership.

Specialists being trained to establish Self-Reliance Groups
for their church in Kinshasa, Congo

These volunteer self-reliance coaches are then invited to a multi-day training session by Interweave. They are given the curriculum and are trained in the "Six P's", as well as how to teach and organize self-reliance groups. There is also training on how to make field visits to monitor small businesses.

Once the volunteer coaches are trained, the congregations announce that they are setting up self-reliance groups in the area and invite their members and friends to the orientation meeting in which the groups will be established.

Interweave was invited to train the micro-finance institution (MFI) called FINCA Costa Rica. In this MFI, the people have created lending groups in which anyone receiving a loan becomes an associate. The associates meet on a monthly basis and conduct business, which includes repaying their loans. The groups have a president and local leadership.

Local FINCA Costa Rica Loan Officers Training
on the 6 P's of Business

Interweave held a two-day training seminar with selected MFI presidents and FINCA Costa Rica loan officers. The training included the Three Circles of Self-Reliance and mentoring in the community. The presidents then had the opportunity to train their groups. They already had regular meetings, but now they had a curriculum and support to help their members improve their businesses, lives, and communities.

In either approach, the goal is to provide a structure and knowledge on how to help people help themselves. With a curriculum and a group format in which adults can counsel together to solve personal and local problems, people look to solve their own challenges rather than waiting for an outside organization or government to intervene.

Show Me the Money

———

Maria has been making underwear for fifteen years. In a room in the back of her family's humble home in Quito, Ecuador she has two sewing machines. For the last fifteen years Maria has struggled to have enough material to get ahead. With the little amount she makes, she buys small amounts of material, makes some clothes, sells them, and buys a little more material to repeat the process.

Maria also never kept books. If she sold an undergarment and had the money in her pocket, it was available money. If the children got sick or rice was needed, then the money would be used. She never was sure how much money she made and never seemed to get ahead.

Then Maria joined a self-reliance association. For the first time in fifteen years she began to record her business income and expenses. She separated her business and personal money, and she began to brand her products. Maria was no longer selling underwear; she was selling "Daisy" undergarments for women and "Tom Steel" briefs for men. Demand began to increase.

Maria was in a position to expand the business and really make it grow, but she needed capital. With a business loan, she could buy material at a cheaper price, buy labels for her garments, and put them in designed boxes instead of cheap plastic bags. She needed money, and she was prepared to invest it.

One of the biggest challenges that come with micro-business development is how to obtain the money to start or grow the small business.

Banks, especially in developing countries, generally do not make micro-business loans. They require a business to be already established, with profit and loss statements, collateral, and years of profitability. People with no formal business records, training, or assets are not a sensible business risk for a formal bank.

In the past thirty years, another financial institution has emerged called a micro-finance institution or MFI. Recognizing the need for smaller loans to new individuals, MFIs are organized to give micro-loans.

MFIs also need to have the loans repaid. They assume the same risk that a bank would have when they offer a loan. How do they establish credit?

The most commonly used method is called village banks. A village bank is a group of people organized to obtain credit from an MFI. The people in the group will guarantee the repayment of the loans given to the individuals in that group. If Maria borrows $400 and is having a hard time paying it back, then the group helps pay back the loan. The entire group is responsible for the repayment of Maria's loan.

MFIs form village banks. The people in the groups then borrow the money and meet once or twice a month to repay the loan money. Everyone with a loan must attend and make his or her loan payment. The MFI loan officer attends the meeting and collects the payment from all of the members. If one of the members doesn't pay, the group makes the payment and then works with the member to pay back the group.

There are several challenges with this model. The obvious one is that people don't like to pay for someone else's loan. If enough people don't pay, then the group collapses, and everyone defaults.

Some MFIs require collateral. A radio, TV, or car is committed. If the individual or group does not pay, the radio is taken as payment.

In many developing countries, a credit score is now available. If someone has borrowed money before and not repaid, then he or she has a low credit score. The MFIs can now look at a potential village bank group and find out the credit score of each of its members. Then they can choose which of these members can receive credit and which cannot. This can have a divisive effect on the group and its members when everyone in the neighborhood knows each other's credit scores.

In Nicaragua, a lady tried to organize a village bank to obtain credit for a small jewelry business she wanted to organize. She had to have ten people to form the group. She invited ten ladies from her church group. After organizing, they found that five of them did not have good credit scores. She invited five more, and three of them didn't have acceptable credit scores. It took her months to try to organize a group before she finally decided it was too difficult and gave up.

Another challenge is that the MFIs must charge a high level of interest to be self-sustaining. Since they are loaning small amounts, $50 to $500, they cannot make much money on each loan. The MFIs have to push as many loans as possible on people who might not need them and have to charge the highest interest rate the market will allow.

It is not uncommon to see an interest rate of 4 percent a month, plus fees. That can be an annualized rate of almost 50 percent for a loan. In the United States we get angry at credit card rates of 18 percent. In developing countries an 18 percent interest rate would be a great bargain.

There are thousands of MFIs in the world. Almost every area of the world has access to at least one. In most areas of the world, there is competition for the best loans available. Each MFI has its own interest rate, fees, and payback plans. Each one has its own system of how it uses groups or how it uses collateral and credit scores. Understanding the structure of the local available MFIs is an important part of helping people become self-reliant.

The first step to obtaining business capital is to know the MFIs in the local area and to evaluate each one. The Interweave coaches train the leaders to study each MFI and try to make a relationship with one or two that can be beneficial to the individuals in the group. Often, credit can be taken care of at the local level, and Interweave or outside organizations don't have to be involved in the loan process.

In some cases, however, MFI loans are impossible to obtain, or have terms that are so onerous that it would be unwise for the struggling small business owner to participate. Loan sharks are known for charging a punishing interest rate with terrible repayment terms. Several MFIs are bordering on, or have become loan sharks.

In this case, Interweave has offered a small loan fund to self-reliance associations in certain countries. The association must have a savings plan to which people will contribute five or ten dollars a month. During that time, they learn the Six P's of Business, set personal goals, and provide community service. Once the association has enough savings and has prepared businesses, members can ask for a loan from Interweave. Interweave will offer four times what members have saved as an association. The association will then put its savings in a special account as a guarantee of that loan.

For example, if twenty members of an association have saved a total of $1,000 and are willing to use that savings as collateral, then Interweave will loan that group $4,000. The loan goes to the association. The association leadership then distributes the loan money among its members. The members pay back the loan to the association, and the association makes the monthly payments on the $4,000. Once that amount of money is paid back, then their original $1,000 in savings is available to the members again. They have an opportunity for another round of borrowing if they choose.

The interest rate that Interweave charges the association is a simple 1 percent a month or 12 percent a year, which helps to pay for the local self-reliance coach in the area. However, the association can charge an interest rate that is closer to the local MFI market rate to its own members if it wishes. If the rate is 4 percent a month plus origination fees, the association can charge 4 percent with no origination fees and then keep 3 percent for its own loan fund or savings. With that potential profit to the associations, once it pays back the loan received from Interweave, it will have a larger pool of savings that the association can leverage for another loan.

A Zimbabwe Group learns more about a Group Loan

So, if the self-reliance association in Bolaro, Zimbabwe has $500 in savings, for example, it can obtain a loan four times greater than its savings, or $2,000 from Interweave at 1 percent a month interest. The Bolaro Association then loans ten members $200 each at 4 percent a month interest over one year, so each member pays back $296 that year. When the ten members have all paid the money back, then the association has collected $2,960. The association repays Interweave the $2,000 plus 1 percent a month interest or $2,240 for the year.

The association now has made a profit of $720 for that year. It has now doubled its savings pool. Instead of $500 in savings, members now have $1,220 as collateral that they leverage again with Interweave for four times the amount, or $4,880 in loan money. If they choose not to continue lending, they can return all of the money back to the association members. However, if they keep saving and keep making money on their loans, the association can be a strong source of small business capital for its members.

The challenge with this model is that the individual members have to pay back the loans. If a member defaults, the local association leadership must secure repayment. They must collect on collateral or work as a group to pay the loan back. If they fail to pay Interweave back, they lose their savings and their ability to help themselves in the future. Some groups have failed to pay back the loans and have lost their savings and the potential to receive loans as a group in the future.

This model has also been successful. First, it requires members to begin to save. This helps with their financial discipline and makes them put some "skin in the game," which is one of the business principles. Second, it challenges the organization to develop leadership and solidarity. The group members must work together and support each other as they decide which loans should be given and which members are ready to seek a loan. The leadership is local, and very good people are helping very good people at the local as well as the international level. Third, when people get the loans, they have previously gone through the Six P's of Business and are more likely to be successful in their business efforts.

Interweave is working to combine business principles with the values of charity. We describe it as "charity with a bottom line and business with a heart." For people to be successful, they must be self-reliant. If they depend on themselves for savings, collection, and business training, then they become groups of motivated people helping each other. The Interweave international donors have provided working capital and not just charity. Their donations keep on giving for years to come as the loans are paid out and collected and businesses are improved.

Interweave gives loans very sparingly. We found that some of the people would join the Interweave program with the only intent of getting money. We want them to focus on the implementation of the 6ps as a goal in and of itself instead of hoping that the end of the process is money.

One business in Congo came to the first Interweave training meeting asking how he could get money for his business. I visited his small dry cleaning operation and I saw that he wasn't ready to take on the burden of a loan repayment. His process to check in the customers clothing was confusing and disorganized. He had no books and was not keeping track of his income and expenses. His promotion consisted of a painted wall that said "Dry Cleaning".

He had no pricing strategy and no written plans in place. If he had received money without going through the discipline of implementing the 6ps in his business, especially keeping simple business records, he would have been saddled with more debt and no growth.

Many Interweave participants have thanked us for not providing them a loan. They found they were progressing with the implementation of the business principles and were enjoying success without the burden of a high interest rate loan repayment. When businesses have implemented the 6ps in their business then they are ready, if they have a specific plan on how to use the loan money, to seek a loan at a local MFI.

Self-Reliance Associations
in the United States

———

Can self-reliance associations work in the United States and other developed countries? Absolutely.

Jorge is experiencing poverty in the United States. He came from Peru six years ago from a teaching position in Lima. He hasn't been able to find stable work since arriving in the U.S.

Because he lives with his adult son, he has a roof overhead and food to eat, but he is still experiencing the pain of poverty and unemployment. His inability to speak English fluently makes finding a job difficult. He never considered starting his own business, until now.

We started a Spanish-speaking self-reliance group in Ogden, Utah and began one in Syracuse, New York (we sometimes call them Prosperity Groups in the United States). The group in Ogden was organized in conjunction with a local community college and the Ogden school district. We held meetings weekly in which Latino parents gathered to discuss small business techniques, local personal goals, and community plans for the future. Speaking in Spanish, parents were able to express their concerns and challenges and, as a group, help each other with suggestions and support.

The membership was diverse. We had a DJ and party planner, an insurance salesman, a businessman who repairs mufflers, two participants who are selling tamales and tres leches, and several who aren't quite sure what they want to do improve their income.

Several started new businesses. Others are keeping accurate records for the first time. Several tried new promotional ideas and pricing schemes. Others decided that business is not for them, but they still enjoyed the group. The sixteen-year-old son of one of the members joined the group to help improve his resume and learn about business and community issues.

In the United States, people can find formal employment easier than in developing countries so the emphasis of the group often moves from small business development to other ways that they and their families can be successful financially. The topic of education and how to succeed in the U.S. education system has become an important issue in self-reliance groups in the United States. Interweave has now developed *Success! in Education: Parent Self Reliance Groups* curriculum in Spanish and English. Success in education for their children is the reason parents get involved at first but soon the discussions will also be about income, improving the home and serving the community.

Since implementing the Ogden and Syracuse self-reliance groups we have established self-reliance groups in several high schools and Junior high schools. The parents start by using our *Success! in Education* manual in which the group teaches each other education terms, how to navigate the school system, how to get involved, how to help their child in school, etc. They choose their own topics to discuss as well which often includes business and income.

Kearns High in Salt Lake City has a dynamic group that has been meeting each week for months. They have discussed everything from bullying and budgeting to stocks and vaccines. The group sets the agenda and helps each other get ahead in life.

Maria is one of their great success stories. She speaks very little English and only went to primary school in Mexico. After having moved to the United States eight years ago she wanted her child to succeed but didn't know how. She explained once that she was so intimidated by the parent nights in the school that she sat outside the school and cried instead of meeting her child's teachers.

That has all changed. She joined the self-reliance group, which speaks Spanish. She has an opportunity to discuss her fears with other parents. They give her ideas and confidence. She began to take assignments in the group including leading the group discussion and visiting other schools to help them organize self-reliance groups. She participates in the service projects and parent fundraisers. Most importantly, she attends her parent teacher conferences and communicates with the teachers now. She has confidence.

The Role of Education in the U.S. Self-Reliance Groups

One of the biggest challenges in the U.S. is the education gap between whites and minorities. Eduardo Ochoa, Assistant Secretary of Education, reported "38% of low-income students move directly to college while 81% of higher-income students move directly to higher education."

Several of the members in these groups have children who have dropped out or are getting low grades. One of the reasons for this gap is the lack of understanding of the U.S. education system. To help solve this problem in the Latino culture, Interweave Solutions made a DVD and started a radio program called El Grito De La Prosperidad (Shout for Prosperity). The title is based on Mexico's Miguel Hidalgo's cry for independence in 1810, an event that is celebrated every September 16th all over the world. His cry was a call to action and so is the radio show and DVD.

The DVD, in Spanish, explains the U.S. education system, defines education terms, talks about how to apply for Free Application for Federal Student Aid (FAFSA), and how to get involved. The Spanish-speaking radio program brings in guest speakers and addresses the same issues. Business challenges and community problems are also discussed. (See ElGritoDeLaProsperidad.org or ShoutForProsperity.org for radio program and DVD information.) El Grito De La Prosperidad DVD and radio show are resources for the Parent Prosperity Groups.

In one of the meetings, we discussed the education gap between Latino students and other ethnic groups. Following the FAMA technique outlined in previous chapters, we showed parents the DVD "El Grito de la Prosperidad" and asked them what they saw in the video. They discussed the education gap, related to it, and identified with it. When asked what they could do to resolve the problem, they decided to start by educating their children about college. We arranged a field trip to Weber State University in Ogden, Utah. Three of the fathers even got off work early and took their children on a tour of the college campus.

I heard a father talking to his daughter and saying, "Do you want to go to college? You will be the first person in the family with a college education."

She proudly said, "Yes, I want to go." Goals had been set, and a commitment was being made.

Fathers with their children at Weber State University

Another father has contacted his child's high school and arranged tutoring for his son. The son's grades went from all Ds and Fs to As and Bs and two Cs this year.

Attending the self reliance groups and listening to our Latino Education Broadcast gave this father the courage to get involved with his son's education in an English Speaking school.

These Latino parents are beginning to find a voice and to show confidence in how to solve their personal challenges.

Parent involvement in the education of their children is one of the great advantages that self-reliance groups can provide in the United States.

Formal education has a major impact on all three circles of self-reliance: income, business, and community.

Self-reliance groups help parent school involvement

Getting a parent to volunteer in school can be difficult. I remember discussing volunteering in the PTA with one parent, and she responded, "All they want me to do is raise more money for the band. I have enough to do without having to sell cookies at school activities."

In fact, the image of "volunteering equals a bake sale" is so common that Anne Henderson and her colleagues wrote a book on parent involvement called *Beyond the Bake Sale*. With self-reliance associations, we are going way beyond the bake sale and teaching a technique that will truly increase parental volunteerism.

When parents truly get involved, they want to have a voice and contribute in meaningful ways. When they feel empowered and have a sense of ownership, they will make powerful contributions to the school, their own homes and the community.

I have attended many school parent meetings, and I have noticed several trends. One is low attendance, especially of minority parents. The parents who do attend are usually quiet and sit on foldout chairs in the rows found in the classroom or in the cafeteria. They quietly listen to what the educators tell them and then enjoy the pizza and refreshments if offered.

One principal in Kentucky bought a 42-inch flat-screen, high-definition TV. She called the parents of the school, told them they were invited to come and get a chance to win a free TV—the kids were not invited. She also used her own money (supposedly) to purchase the TV to get them there. On the night of the meeting, she raffled it off to parents who came to a meeting. She then told her personal story of how she finished school as an adult and is now the principal. The event was a wild success in terms of attendance, but was it a success in terms of involvement?

If we want parents to contribute time to the school, then we need to give them a voice. We need to give them an opportunity to speak up and discuss a problem or issue and offer solutions. People are often reluctant to participate in group discussions, especially those who dropped out of school themselves, and are uncomfortable with institutions or with the language.

Self-reliance groups give parents a reason to leave the house and participate in the community. Parents come to the meetings because they are talking about something that can influence their pocketbook as well as their child's education. They are learning about business, employment, and setting personal goals and are not just there to be told what the school needs. Self-reliance groups using the FAMA technique have a powerful impact on parent involvement in the community.

In each of the international service examples I have shared, the parents set the agenda and resolved local community problems while improving their businesses and homes. That is now happening in the United States. U.S. groups have had community fund raisers to provide Latino scholarships, provide backpacks and supplies and to help the local libraries. They are inviting other parents that have previously been isolated immigrants or uninvolved parents and teaching them how to navigate the school system and apply principles of self-reliance. Self reliance groups work in the United States.

So What Do We Do?

———

I think we all have a bit of charity in us that wants to help solve the poverty and injustice in the world, but we just don't know how. We are grateful for our two sinks in our bathrooms. We know that ripping one of them out will not improve anyone's income or quality of life. So what do we do?

My daughter and I were talking about what we should do if a friend or acquaintance asks us for money or help. When do we help? Will money help?

We are offered many ways to give on a regular basis. Many non-profit organizations offer food, hot meals, clean water, school buildings, or disaster relief. Often, friends who always seem to be in trouble ask for help. These charities are valuable and should be supported, and these friends may be needy, but always remember the importance of self-reliance. I am inviting you to reserve part of your help and donations to organizations that encourage self-reliance, and when you give to friends and relatives, please keep self-reliance in mind.

In order to determine whether your help or donation encourages self-reliance, you can ask two important questions:

1. Does the donation help or encourage some sort of income generation?
2. Is the recipient of the donation, to the extent possible, asked to work, contribute to, or purchase something to receive the service?

Do you or the nonprofit organization encourage income generation?

Be careful of giveaway charities or handouts. Even though they provide much needed immediate relief, they can have a long-term disruptive effect on income generation.

Whether it be reading glasses, mosquito nets, or used clothing, if a well-meaning organization or individual gives away products or services without thinking about how the recipient will earn a living in the future, it often creates a longer-term problem of dependency.

I remember talking to a seamstress of thirty years in El Salvador who was trying to create a new business because she said she could not compete with the flood of used clothes on the market. Charity had destroyed her business.

Doctors have often given services for free. They will go into a village and perform life-saving operations. They must be encouraged, however, to think about the income-generation component when they leave.

In a poor area of Port-au-Prince, a European NGO came and offered free medical services for about a year. Everyone was excited about the high quality of care from the Europeans. Any local doctors in the area could not compete against the free care offered, and they left that section of the city. A year later the Europeans pulled out of Haiti. The area was left without local health care, and the people in the neighborhood were at the mercy of government or international NGOs to solve their local problem. Charity had caused dependency and destroyed local initiative.

The European doctor group should have had a focus on training local doctors with not only medical practices but also with business ideas for how to provide these services when they were gone. They should have helped local doctors price their services, promote the services, and improve the local process. They should have taught them what products or services would be included in treatment and how to develop a long-term growth plan. Local doctors need to know the Six P's of Business.

Please, in your donating, look for organizations that have an income-generating component. Is there small business training? Is there a micro-lending fund? Is there local leadership and involvement in the project? All of these are important questions when looking for a donation that will make a long-term impact on self-reliance.

When working with a friend or relative, have the discussion about long-term solutions. Perhaps make the person commit to attending a career workshop, self reliance group or register at workforce services as a condition of receiving your help.

Do you or the nonprofit organization invite the recipients to work, contribute to, or purchase, to the extent possible, the product or service?

Another harmful result of just giving away nets or glasses or medicine is that it often goes unappreciated or unused. If the recipient hasn't gone through the thought process of the value of a net and made the sacrifice to purchase one, then he or she often puts it to the side and neglects it.

I visited a home of a family in drought-stricken Ethiopia. A well-meaning NGO had built a rain collection system with a 500-gallon tank on a poor woman's farm. When we visited, the connection from the roof to the gallon container was missing. She had taken the spout for another use. The collection system was inoperative one month after installation. She had not processed the value of the water collection system and had not participated in its development. She was pleased that some outsider had come and done some work on the farm, but she had not put in her efforts to make the system succeed.

Any behavior change, whether it is wearing glasses, sleeping in nets, or collecting water in a new way, needs to be accepted and processed by the local villager. There has to be a "conversion" to the idea. Selling a product or service is an excellent way to create buy-in. An economic transaction offers an opportunity for the purchaser to commit to the product or service. The person has to be educated enough to understand the purchase and committed enough to make the purchase.

If we encourage local villagers to sell goods and services at reasonable prices and teach them how to make a profit in the process, then we have a win-win-win situation. Jobs are created, services in the community are provided, and end-users are persuaded and committed to use the product.

What if the person doesn't have the money to pay? This is often true of an education, a well, a house, or other larger ticket items. In this case, offering some form of meaningful work or service as a "payment" is an important part of self-reliance. The recipient should help dig the latrine, help gather the people, sell the glasses, provide referrals, or give leadership. The local participant needs to do all he or she can to "purchase" or earn the product or service.

The local villagers asking for latrines, schools, books, or water wells should also be able to explain their local commitment to the project. Do they have a local leadership council that is advocating for the project? Are they encouraging local participation? Are they requiring local commitment?

I was talking to an engineer who wanted to make a difference in the world. He went on a service expedition to Africa. He found himself in a hole digging a new latrine next to another professional businessman who was digging with him. They looked around and saw the villagers watching the curious sight of the two white men digging the hole. He suddenly realized that the one thing that these villagers could offer in this project was labor. They had time, curiosity, and ability to dig a hole, yet they stood around watching. Self-reliance is fostered when we challenge and invite the recipients to do as much of the planning, work, and implementation as possible.

When giving money to a friend or family member, try to ask them to do something for the money. Maybe they can develop a family budget, clean their own kitchen, or help you with some yard work before they receive the money they need or want. Try to help them do all they can to earn or work for the donation.

So when deciding whether to give to a project or organization, two good questions to ask are:

> *Does this charity help the people being served to generate their own income?*

> *Is this donation challenging the recipients to work or contribute to improve their own cause?*

Think self-reliance.

InterweaveSolutions.org

Good people help good people solve their own poverty through self-reliance groups.

InterweaveSolutions.org is dedicated to helping people become self-reliant. It features projects from around the world in which people solve their own problems, teach each other business principles, and help set their own improvement goals.

The website is updated regularly. There are wonderful stories of people and groups solving their local problems and providing service in their own communities. The service projects and businesses are as varied as the people.

Service has included killing the snakes and cutting the grass in Zimbabwe to visiting old folk's homes in Ecuador. Orphanages have been painted, streets cleaned, and gardens grown and harvested, all in an effort to solve local problems without government or international involvement.

Hairdressers, artisans, gardeners, shopkeepers, and clothes makers have all improved their sources of income by learning and teaching the Six P's of Business. Record keeping, promotion plans, branding ideas, and pricing plans have all been implemented. Many have taught each other. Their classes are now ongoing in the community.

Personal goals are being set. People quit drinking, attend church, or make peace with their spouses. People are saving money for the first time and are keeping personal budgets. The groups are helping individuals improve their own businesses, homes, and communities.

You can specifically help create self-reliance in three ways at Interweave Solutions.

First, sponsor a country. Working together in a country of your choice and with your generous sponsorship and involvement, we would hire a local in that country. He or she would then work with local churches, schools, NGOs and other groups that want to help people become self reliant. With Interweave training and supplies along with your vision could help hundreds become self-reliant.

Second, sponsor an organization. We often get requests from organizations that hear about us in developing countries. They want to start groups but can't afford the materials and training. You could provide those materials.

We were once contacted by an NGO in Africa that needed help with self-reliance. About 250 girls had been kidnapped six years ago by rebel armies in Uganda. Used as sex slaves, these girls spent the next six years in the rebel camps. The war is now over and these young women with their children are being dumped and deserted on the roads of Uganda. The NGO wants to help with immediate demands but needs to have a long-term plan for income generation for these families. Simple small business techniques, group support and goal getting through self-reliance groups should be an important part of that long-term strategy. You could provide an NGO like this with the supplies necessary to start those groups.

Finally, provide a self-reliance scholarship. For very little money, a young mother in Tampico, Mexico or Kinshasa, Congo could start a group. But they may not belong to a local organization and therefore have no way to get started. Through the Interweave scholarship program, they can apply for materials that you purchased and get a local group going. Even a small contribution can provide a participant handbook for someone who wants to participate in a group but doesn't have the money.

Someone in Choluteca, Honduras once contacted us. They were ready to start a group but they couldn't afford materials. Through your scholarship contribution, we could provide materials for them to establish their own self-reliance group. Don't worry. We will encourage them to provide service to their community so that they can earn that scholarship!

Read about it on the website. Sponsor a country, sponsor an organization and/or provide a scholarship. Experience self-reliance at Interweavesolutions.org.

It Can Be Done

Whether you have two sinks or not, if you have ever wondered what you could do to help relieve the poor, you are not alone. There are millions of people like you worldwide.

When you give to organizations that are focused on self-reliance, you are making a long-term difference. When *local* people are working with each other in self-reliance groups, and you have helped provide the training and support to make it happen, then together you are positively impacting their homes, businesses, and communities at the grassroots level.

You now have a vehicle to work with people worldwide. We invite you to be part of the Interweave movement. Let's put a self-reliance group in every poor area of the world. Let's work together, charity with a bottom line, business with a heart- to help people lift themselves out of poverty.

www.InterweaveSolutions.org

ABOUT THE AUTHOR

———

Dean H. Curtis is the chairman and co-founder of Interweave Solutions, a non-profit organization that has created over one hundred self-reliance groups worldwide and developed materials to help Latinos succeed in education in the United States.

Prior to creating Interweave Solutions, Dean was a successful entrepreneur who established and sold a business with over 500 employees, was a former Assistant Professor of Communication and Business at the University of Nebraska, Kearney, and taught high school in Spanish Fork, Utah.

Dean completed his Ph.D. coursework at the University of Nebraska, Lincoln (starting a business instead of writing a dissertation) and has a masters and bachelor's degree from Brigham Young University.

Dean and his wife have served their church with their family on a three year mission to Tampico, Mexico. They are the parents of nine children. Dean has traveled worldwide, teaching principles of self-reliance.